LET'S GET THIS PARTY STARTED!

Slumber Party Ideas, Snacks, Games
and Other Cool Stuff

Printed in China.

Distributed By:

700 Woodlands Parkway
Vernon Hills, IL 60061
ISBN-13: 978-1-56383-239-0
ISBN-10: 1-56383-239-9

Table of Contents

Girls Night 1

Spa Night 11

Fiesta... 19

Western 27

Luau 35

Campout 43

Movie Star Night 51

Sports Party 59

Mardi Gras 67

Spooky Party................................... 75

Rock & Roll Party............................. 83

Beach Party 91

70's Night 99

Party Planner............................... 107

Girls Night

Congratulations
You're throwing a Slumber Party!

A lot of the fun comes in the planning and preparation for the party. In this book you'll find lots of ideas for theme parties, as well as this Girls Night section, which includes general Slumber Party ideas. Let's start with the invitations…

Party Invitations

Go on, let your mind go crazy with ideas and don't be afraid to get creative! If you are planning a special activity, such as a swim party or roller skating party, don't forget to include those details on the invitations. Make sure that everyone knows what they will need to bring, whether it is only pajamas and a pillow, or sleeping bags, swimsuits, roller skates, extra money, etc. Also, be sure to include the date, address and time the party will start.

Pajama Invitations

What makes you think of a Pajama Party more than flannel? Cover heavyweight paper with a flannel material found at your local fabric or crafts store and write the party details on the inside of the card. Or sew the fabric into a pillow shape and stuff the filled-out invitation inside the pillow.

Orange Creamsicles

Makes 4 servings

4 C. orange juice
12 scoops vanilla
  frozen yogurt

1 orange, cut into
  round slices

In a blender or food processor, pour orange juice. Scoop ice cream into blender. Process on high until mixture is creamy. Pour into tall glasses and garnish each serving with an orange wheel.

Make Your Own Pizzas

Prepare or purchase a small single-serving cheese pizza for every guest. Fill the table with fun pizza toppings, such as pepperoni, Canadian bacon, tomatoes, green peppers, black olives, pineapple and sausage. Let each guest create their own pizza by adding their favorite toppings. Bake pizzas according to package directions, or until cheese is melted and crust is golden brown.

Sleeping Bag & Pillow Treats

Makes 6 treats

1½ C. powdered sugar
3 to 6 T. milk
Food coloring

Whole and partial
graham crackers

Place ½ cup powdered sugar in each of three separate bowls. Add 1 to 2 tablespoons milk to each bowl and stir until mixture is smooth. Place a few drops food coloring in each bowl and stir until desired color is achieved. Use plastic knives to spread frosting over graham crackers and decorate to look like sleeping bags and pillows. These are a fun treat to display and eat at your slumber party!

Party Pillows

Purchase a cheap, white pillow case for each guest (or sew them out of white fabric). Gather fabric markers, puff paints, extra fabric, buttons and decorations and let each guest decorate their own pillow case. Slip a piece of cardboard between the pillowcases so the paint or ink doesn't sink through to the other side as they are decorated. Set the pillowcases out to dry overnight and let each guest take their pillowcase home with them as a party favor and reminder of a great party!

Caramel Corn

Makes 4 quarts

3 qts. popcorn, popped
3 C. dry-roasted, unsalted
   mixed nuts
1 C. brown sugar
½ C. light corn syrup

½ C. margarine
½ tsp. salt
½ tsp. baking soda
½ tsp. vanilla

Preheat oven to 250°. In a large roasting pan, combine popped popcorn and nuts. Place in oven while preparing glaze. In a medium saucepan, combine brown sugar, corn syrup, margarine and salt. Remove from heat and stir in baking soda and vanilla. Pour glaze over warm popcorn and nuts, tossing to coat well. Bake another 60 minutes, stirring every 10 to 15 minutes. Cool and break apart. Store in an airtight container.

Slumber Party Videos

Make sure to have videos ready for the time when everyone starts to quiet down and get tired (but isn't ready to go to bed yet)! Some classic slumber party movies are:

Sixteen Candles
Parent Trap
Never Been Kissed
Harry Potter
Mrs. Doubtfire
Ferris Bueller's Day Off

The Sound of Music
Wild Hearts Can't
  Be Broken
Can't Buy Me Love
Adventures in Babysitting
Sleepless in Seattle

Quiz:

Does Your Crush Like You Too?

1. When you see "your guy" at the mall with his friends, he usually:
    - **A.** Walks right past you. You're not even sure he noticed you at all.
    - **B.** Gives you a small smile, nods and says "hey".
    - **C.** Bumps your arm, trying to make you drop your bags.

2. Your science teacher just paired you and your crush up for a project. When you meet him at the lab station, he:
    - **A.** Doesn't look up, he's too engrossed with the microscope.
    - **B.** Turns about 14 shades of red and says "Um, hi."
    - **C.** Jokes, "Oh, no! We're totally going to fail!"

3. You decided to chop all your hair off and you love it! When your crush sees you for the first time, he:
    - **A.** Looks confused, like he knows you look different but can't quite figure out why.
    - **B.** Smiles and says he likes your hair.
    - **C.** Teases you non-stop.

4. Whenever you run into him outside the confines of school, it's usually:
    - **A.** A coincidence. But it's gonna happen 'cause you both hang at the same places.
    - **B.** A total surprise. You've still not been able to figure out how his bike got a flat in your driveway.
    - **C.** At a great party or game – he hasn't missed one yet!

5. You make a terrible joke and everyone in the room groans. Your crush:
    - **A.** Changes the subject.
    - **B.** Laughs like it's the funniest thing he's ever heard.
    - **C.** Groans louder than anyone else and even repeats the joke mimicking you to a tee.

Find out if he's crushing on you too!
If you answered the questions
on the previous page with:

Mostly A's…
 This guy holds all his feelings deep inside and doesn't give any hints. Of course, he might be too into his buds to care about crushes right now. But, there's a chance he's really into you and is just too shy to actually act on his romantic impulses. If you want to find out for sure, try to draw him out of his shell and get a conversation going. You'll probably have to be bold and not only make the first move, but lots of them to find out how he feels!

Mostly B's…
 This guy's got it bad for you. He hangs on your every word and feels lucky just to spend time with you – all your friends and even his pals know it! The next step is to move past the crush stage and onto an actual date. All you've got to do is continue being you. Once he's totally confident you'll say yes (because he's been getting that steady stream of positive signals from you) he'll be on the phone, email or smoke signal, asking you out!

Mostly C's…
 This guy is super-charismatic, so it's no wonder he's the hit of every party! While he may value you as a friend, he's not seeing you as potential girlfriend material. Try showing him that you're more than just a bud. If things don't work out, don't sweat it too much. This guy is such a social butterfly that it might take him a long time to finally settle down with anyone. In the meantime, there's another cutie right around the bend that's waiting just for you!

Palm Reading

Have your guests place their right hand, palm side up, in front of you and amaze them by reading what their hand reveals about them. The right hand reveals how you deal with other people on a daily basis, whether they are your friends, family, schoolmates or acquaintances. If the lines in the palm are wavy, non-continuous lines, or the skin is tight, it is a good indication that past experiences are still affecting your everyday life.

Strong, straight fingers and deep, clear lines indicate that you are in good condition to face whatever lies ahead. You are better prepared to handle outer world problems.

20 Questions

Choose one person in the group to think of a person, place or thing and write it down on a piece of paper. Make sure they hide the paper from everyone else! All the other guests have to try to figure out the person, place or thing that was written on the paper by asking only 20 questions or less.

The questions can only be answered with a "Yes" or "No". If someone thinks they know the answer, they can use up one of the questions by saying what they think the answer is. If that person is correct, they get to think of the next person, place or thing and write it down.

Grabbit

Start this game by placing small objects on the table to use as prizes, for example; a book, a bag of candy, a CD or nail polish. Have every player name their favorite card game.

Remove all but one of the prizes from the table. This will be the prize that everyone is playing for. Play one of the card games listed by the guests and the winner gets to keep the prize that is on the table. Replace with another prize and play the next card game.

Truth or Dare

Make all of your guests sit in a circle. Choose one person to begin. This person sits in the middle of the circle and everyone else asks "Truth or Dare". The person then must respond by either choosing to tell a "Truth" or do a "Dare". If she responds by saying "Truth", then everyone else gets to decide one question to ask that person. She must respond by answering the question truthfully. If she responds by saying "Dare", then she must perform the dare that is presented to her by everyone else. Take turns being the person in the middle.

Spoons

You will need one deck of cards without Jokers. You will also need one less spoon than the amount of players, for example: 4 spoons for 5 players, 9 spoons for 10 players, etc. The object of this game is to collect four matching cards (4 aces, 4 sevens, etc.) and to not be the person left without a spoon.

Place the spoons in the middle of the table, making sure they are within grabbing distance of all players. Deal 4 cards to each player and the dealer keeps the deck. The dealer starts the game by picking up 1 card from the deck, deciding if he or she wants to keep it and passing it on. If any player decides to keep the passed card, they must discard 1 card from their hand, making sure to only have 4 cards at a time. The dealer continues passing cards around the circle.

Once one player has four of a kind, he or she can grab a spoon from the pile. Once someone has grabbed a spoon from the pile, the rest of the players are free to grab a spoon. The player without a spoon is out of the game. The game continues by eliminating the player without a spoon and 1 spoon from the pile. The cards are reshuffled and dealt. The winner is the last player still alive.

Note: This game is very exciting when the dealer passes the cards as quickly as possible and the player with four of a kind is very discreet when grabbing a spoon. Sometimes players will continue playing for quite a while before realizing there is a missing spoon.

Beauty Rest Invitations

Create invitations in the shape of sleeping eye pillows. Cut the shape out of heavyweight paper and cover the paper or light cardboard with silk fabric. Attach a string. Write the details of the invitation on one side of the sleeping eye pillows.

Cosmetic Bag Invitations

Write the details of the party on a sheet of heavyweight paper and slip it inside a purchased zip-close cosmetic bag for each invitation. You could include travel-size bath and body items inside the cosmetic bag, such as a small bottle of lotion or nail file for each guest. Encourage each guest to bring the cosmetic bag to the party. They can use it to carry home a party favor, or their items acquired in the Lipstick Treasure Hunt on page 18.

Spa Jackets

Purchase a pack of extra-large white men's T-shirts. Cut a vertical line down the front of each T-shirt. Write each guests name in puff paint on the T-shirt pocket and the name of the Spa, for example: Jessie's Day Spa, on the back of the T-shirt using more puff paint or fabric markers. As each guest enters the party, have them slip into their spa jacket and a pair of comfy slippers to get into the mood!

Razzle Dazzle Cocktails

Makes 1 serving

1 frozen banana   1 C. orange juice
¾ C. fresh raspberries

    In a blender, combine frozen banana, fresh raspberries and orange juice. Process on high until evenly blended. Pour into a tall glass and serve.

Apple Slushies

Makes 1 serving

8 apple cider cubes   ¼ C. apple cider

    Prepare apple cider cubes in advance by pouring apple cider into ice cube molds and placing in freezer until solid. In a blender, combine apple cider cubes and apple cider. Process on high until evenly blended. Pour into a glass and serve.

Basic Manicure

Place a medium bowl of warm water in front of every guest. Have everyone rest their fingers and hands in the warm water for 3 minutes, then rub some of the Cocoa Butter Hand and Nail Treatment (recipe below) over their hands, working the moisturizer into the base of each nail. Use a soft cotton cuticle tool to gently push back the cuticles on each finger. Have a nail clipper handy so everyone can trim their nails and remove any jagged edges. Divide into partners and massage more of the Cocoa Butter Hand and Nail Treatment over each other's hands. It's nice to have a partner perform the massage so that one person can relax – and then switch roles. Lightly buff the nails, but be careful not to buff too hard or the nails will burn.

Cocoa Butter Hand and Nail Treatment

2 T. beeswax
2 T. cocoa butter

4 T. jojoba oil
1 T. anhydrous lanolin

In a double boiler over simmering water, combine all ingredients, mixing until completely melted. Remove from heat and let cool until just slightly warm. If desired, mix in a few drops of essential oil. Pour mixture into separate containers and cover with a lid. This mixture will keep for several months and does not need to be refrigerated. If the mixture becomes cold and hardens, warm in the microwave for a few seconds to soften again prior to use.

Homemade Cranberry Lip Gloss

1 T. sweet almond oil   1 tsp. honey
10 fresh cranberries

In a small microwave-safe bowl, combine almond oil, fresh cranberries and honey. Heat in microwave for 2 minutes, or until mixture begins to boil. Remove from microwave and stir until well mixed, gently crushing the berries. Pour the mixture into several small containers through a fine-hole sieve, removing any bits of cranberry skin or seeds. Cover the containers with lids.

Sweet Vanilla Lip Balm

1 tsp. petroleum jelly   1½ tsp. coconut oil
1 tsp. aloe vera gel   ½ tsp. vanilla

In a double boiler over simmering heat, combine petroleum jelly, aloe vera gel, coconut oil and vanilla. Heat, stirring often, until mixture is liquefied. Pour into separate containers and cover with lids.

Spin the Bottle

This is a colorful variation to the regular spin the bottle game. You will need an empty soda bottle and 10 bottles of nail polish, each in a different color.

Set the nail polish in a circle with enough room for the empty bottle to spin in the middle. Have everyone take turns spinning the bottle. Whatever nail polish bottle the empty bottle is pointing at once it stops spinning, is the color that guest must paint one of their fingernails. Continue playing until everyone has painted each of their 10 fingernails. See the colorful and crazy combinations that everyone ends up with!

No Mirror Make-Up

This is a hilarious game that gets everyone laughing. Set out lots of beauty products on a table and have everyone apply their make-up without using a mirror. The person who has the most hideous look is the winner! Make sure to have a camera handy so you can take photos of everyone with their crazy make-up on!

Funky Face Mask

¼ C. powdered clay   3 tsp. cornstarch

Combine the above mixture for each face mask. Depending on what type of mask you would like to do, add the following oils.

For a Rejuvenating Face Mask: add 1 teaspoon peppermint essential oil, 1 teaspoon jasmine essential oil and 1 teaspoon calendula essential oil (or a mixture of these to equal 3 teaspoons) to the above mixture.
For a Relaxing Face Mask: add 3 drops sandalwood essential oil, 3 drops lavender essential oil and 2 drops calendula essential oil (or a mixture of these to equal 8 drops) to the above mixture.
For Dry Skin: add 4 teaspoons sweet almond or jojoba oil to the above mixture.
For Oily Skin: add 4 teaspoons brewers yeast to the above mixture.

Now, stir in enough water, 1 tablespoon at a time, to form a paste. Rub the mixture gently over your face and let it dry. After about 5 to 10 minutes, rinse your face with warm water and pat dry with a clean towel.

Lipstick Games

Lipstick Treasure Hunt

Make a list of five bath and body products that are hidden around the house for each guest. Make sure there are five different items for each person, and write out the different lists of those items. Try to be as specific as you can when listing the products. For example, on one person's list, she is to find only the blue nail polish, orange cream lip balm, pink raspberry body spray, etc. But on another list, the guest is supposed to find only the bright red nail polish, mint flavored lip gloss, lavender body spray, etc. Give a copy of the list to each player and send them out to collect the items. If the person should happen to find an item that is not on their list, then they have to leave it where it was found. The first one to collect all items on their list is the winner and gets to pick one item from everyone else. This way, everyone else will get to keep four of their items, but the winner is rewarded by getting to keep more.

Best Lips Contest

Have each girl put on a heavy coat of a different lipstick color. Hang a large piece of white poster board on the wall and have each girl take turns planting a big, wet one on the board. Make sure to remember who used what color so you can laugh as you compare the different lip marks left by everyone.

Name That Lipstick

Arrange all the lipsticks on the table and make up new and crazy names for each color. Have fun as everyone tries to remember the names you came up with the next morning.

Fiesta

Taco Invitations

Cut circles out of yellow construction paper and fold in half to make semi-circles. Write the details of the invitation inside the circle and decorate the edges with additional construction paper to look like a taco. Cut strips of green paper to look like lettuce, strips of orange paper to look like shredded cheese, small squares of red paper to look like chopped tomatoes, etc.

Fiesta Invitations

Use other symbols of a typical fiesta to use on your invitations, like a cactus, sombrero, donkey, colorful Mexican blanket or chile pepper. Use bright colored paper to decorate your invitations and write phrases like "Ole", "Mui Bueno" and "Arriba! Arriba! Andale! Andale!" all over them.

Mexicali Popcorn

Makes 10 cups

10 C. popped popcorn
1 tsp. taco seasoning
¼ C. butter, melted

¼ C. shredded Cheddar
and Colby Jack
cheese blend

Place the popped popcorn in a large bowl. In a small bowl, mix together the taco seasoning, melted butter and shredded cheese, stirring until well combined. Pour over the popcorn and toss until evenly incorporated.

Cheesy Quesadilla

Makes 4 servings

4 flour tortillas
1 to 1½ C. shredded
  Cheddar cheese

1 (16 oz.) jar thick n'
  chunky salsa
1 (16 oz.) container
  sour cream

Place 1 tortilla on a microwave-safe plate. Sprinkle about ¼ cup shredded Cheddar cheese over tortilla. Fold tortilla in half and cover with plastic wrap. Microwave on high for 25 to 40 seconds or until the cheese begins to melt. Let stand, covered, for 1 minute. Fold quesadilla in half again. Repeat with remaining tortillas and shredded Cheddar cheese. Serve with salsa and sour cream.

Lime Cooler

Makes 5 servings

¾ C. fresh lime juice   1 qt. water
⅔ C. honey   Lime wedges for garnish

In a large pitcher, combine the lime juice, honey and water. Mix until well combined and honey is completely dissolved. Pour mixture evenly into tall glasses filled with ice. Garnish each serving with a lime wedge.

The Best Guacamole

Makes about 2 cups

2 large ripe avocados   1 tsp. garlic powder
1 Roma tomato   Salt to taste
2 tsp. dried cilantro   Tortilla chips

Peel, pit and dice the avocados. Dice the tomato. In a large bowl, mash the diced avocado and stir in the diced tomato. Season with dried cilantro, garlic powder and salt to taste, stirring until well combined. Serve with tortilla chips for dipping.

Taco Bar

1 lb. ground beef	Sliced olives
1 (1 oz.) pkg. taco seasoning	Salsa
	Chopped green onions
2 T. water	Sour cream
Shredded lettuce	Taco shells
Shredded cheese	Flour tortillas

In a large skillet over medium high heat, cook the ground beef until evenly browned, crumbling into small pieces. Drain the fat from the skillet and stir in the taco seasoning and water. Cook until evenly heated and transfer taco meat to a serving bowl. Place other bowls on the table filled with shredded lettuce, shredded cheese, sliced olives, salsa, chopped green onions and sour cream.

Have each guest build their own tacos by filling either the taco shells or flour tortillas with their favorite toppings!

Super Nachos

Makes 6 servings

1 lb. ground beef
1 onion, finely diced
Salt and pepper to taste
1 (14½ oz.) pkg. tortilla
  chips
1 (16 oz.) can refried
  beans

2 C. shredded
  Cheddar cheese
1 jalapeno pepper,
  sliced, optional

In a large skillet over medium high heat, cook the ground beef and diced onion, stirring often, until beef is browned and onion is softened. Drain fat from skillet and season meat mixture with salt and pepper to taste.

To assemble nachos, arrange tortilla chips on a large serving platter. Place dollops of refried beans over chips. Layer half of the shredded Cheddar cheese and half of the ground beef mixture over the beans. Repeat layers with more chips, more refried beans, remaining cheese and remaining beef mixture. If desired, top with slices of jalapeno pepper.

Make Your Own Piñata

You will need a large balloon for each guest, flour, warm water, newspapers, scissors, colored tissue paper, colored construction paper, white glue, paint brushes, string and candy to fill the piñatas.

Have everyone inflate their balloon and tie it closed. Cut lots of small strips from the newspaper. In a medium bowl, make a paste out of the flour and warm water, using one cup flour for every two cups of water. Dip the newspaper strips into the paste and apply them to the balloon. Continue until the balloon is covered with several layers of the newspaper strips, making sure they cover every surface of the balloon except for the small end where the balloon was tied. Set aside balloons to dry. This may take up to 2 days, so the piñatas could be prepared up to this point and ready for each guest to decorate once they come to the party.

After the layers of newspaper are completely dry, pop the balloon. This will leave a small hole in the piñata. Carefully cut the end off of the piñata around this small hole. Securely tie a long piece of string around a washer or empty spool of thread and stick it inside piñata. Fill the piñata with small prizes or individually wrapped candies. Replace the cut off end and cover again with more strips of newspaper dipped in the paste. Repeat until the hole is completely covered and the long string is sticking out of the piñata, which is being held in place by the spool of thread inside the piñata.

Once the covered end is dry, decorate the piñata with pieces of colored tissue paper and construction paper, attaching with a thin layer of white glue. Hang the piñata by the long piece of string over a tree branch outdoors. Take turns blindfolding the guests and having them swing a stick or baseball bat at the piñata until it bursts open and candy and prizes fall out everywhere!

Sombrero Cookies

Makes 3 dozen

1 C. butter, softened	2 tsp. baking powder
1 C. sugar	¼ C. heavy
2 eggs	whipping cream
1 tsp. vanilla	36 gumdrops
3¾ C. flour	

In a medium bowl, cream together the butter and sugar. Stir in the eggs and vanilla. Into a separate bowl, sift the flour and baking powder. Alternating, stir the flour mixture and heavy cream into the butter mixture. Cover dough with plastic wrap and chill in refrigerator for 2 to 3 hours. Preheat oven to 350° and lightly grease 2 baking sheets. On a lightly floured surface, roll out dough to ¼" thickness and cut into circles with a 2" round cookie cutter. Place cookies 1" apart on the prepared baking sheets. Bake in oven for 12 to 14 minutes, or until bottoms and edges of cookies are lightly browned. Remove from oven and transfer cookies to wire racks to cool completely. Spread icing over cookies and press one gumdrop in the center of each cookie to look like a sombrero.

Cookie Icing

1 C. powdered sugar	¼ tsp. almond extract
2 tsp. milk	Assorted food coloring
2 tsp. light corn syrup	

In a small bowl, combine powdered sugar and milk, mixing until smooth. Whisk in the corn syrup and almond extract, stirring until smooth. If the icing is too thick, stir in a little more corn syrup. Divide icing into separate bowls and add a few drops of food coloring to each bowl.

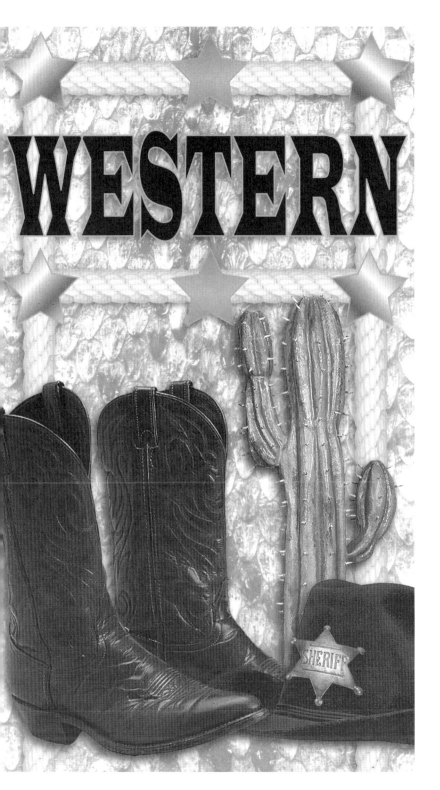

WESTERN

Cowboy Boot Invitations

Cut out paper in the shape of a cowboy boot – use pink paper to give it more of a cowgirl theme! Decorate one side with extravagant designs that look like etchings in the boot. Include the party details on the other side. Encourage everyone to dress in western attire!

Bigger Than Texas Invitations

Throw a Slumber Party that is bigger than Texas! Start by creating invitations in the shape of the state of Texas. Fill in the party details on one side and add a little Texas glitz by decorating the invitations with glitter!

Bandana Invitations

Write the invitations on heavyweight paper and roll them up or wrap them inside a handkerchief. You could use a different colored handkerchief for every guest. Encourage the guests to bring their handkerchief to the party and use them to make Dazzlin' Bandanas, instructions on page 29.

Decorate Cowgirl Hats

This can be a great way to get the party started and provides something for each guest to wear throughout the evening. Have each guest bring a plain, undecorated cowboy hat to the party, or purchase these for all guests at a local toy or crafts store. Also provide lots of little decorative items, including colorful feathers, ribbons, decorative trimming, little plastic flowers or items, buttons, or bandanas to decorate the cowboy hats. Provide a hot glue gun so everyone can attach these items to their hat!

Dazzlin' Bandanas

Another way to get your guests in the western mood is to provide different colored handkerchiefs that everyone can decorate. Provide fake jewels, buttons and accessories that can either be sewed or glued onto the bandana fabric.

Hot Cakes

Makes 12 servings

Prepare these pancakes in advance and keep them in the freezer. In the morning, when everyone is starving for breakfast, just have each guest pop the pancakes in the toaster to heat them up again. Provide yummy toppings like fresh fruit, syrup, whipped cream and chocolate chips to top their pancakes.

3 C. flour
3 T. sugar
3 tsp. baking powder
1½ tsp. baking soda
¾ tsp. salt

3 C. buttermilk
½ C. milk
3 eggs
$^1/_3$ C. butter, melted

In a large bowl, combine flour, sugar, baking powder, baking soda and salt. In a separate bowl, whisk together buttermilk, milk, eggs and melted butter. Preheat a lightly oiled griddle to medium high heat. To tell if the griddle is heated enough, flick water across the surface. If the water beads up and sizzles, the griddle is ready. Pour the wet mixture into the dry mixture and mix with a wooden spoon or fork just until blended, being careful not to overmix. Scoop the batter onto the griddle, ½ cup at a time, and make different pools to form the pancakes. Heat until lightly browned on one side and carefully flip each pancake to cook the other side. Serve hot, or place in a ziplock bag in the freezer until later use.

Southwestern Subs

Makes about 12 servings

2 (11 oz.) pkgs.
  refrigerated French
  bread dough
1/3 C. Thousand Island
  dressing
½ tsp. prepared yellow
  mustard
2 T. chopped green
  peppers

1½ C. shredded lettuce
1 medium tomato, sliced
8 oz. deli roast beef,
  thinly sliced
4 oz. Pepper Jack cheese,
  thinly sliced

Preheat oven to 350°. Place bread dough, seam side down, on a baking sheet. Join the end of the dough together to form one large circle and pinch the ends together to seal. Cut six to eight ½" deep slashes across the top of the dough. Bake dough in oven for 26 to 30 minutes, or until deep golden brown. Remove bread from oven and place on a wire rack to cool completely. Cut bread in half horizontally. In a small bowl, combine Thousand Island dressing, chopped green peppers and mustard, mixing until well combined. Spread sauce over bread and top with shredded lettuce, tomato slices, roast beef slices and Pepper Jack cheese slices. Place top half of bread over sandwich ingredients and cut into slices to serve.

Smiling Cowgirls

This game is guaranteed to get all of your cowgirl guests smiling and laughing. Have everyone stand or sit in a circle with one person in the middle. The person in the middle of the group has to go stand right in front of someone else in the circle and say, "Cowgirl, I love you! Will you please, please smile?"

The person who was asked has to answer back without smiling, "Cowgirl, I love you, but I just can't smile!" If the person can't say it without smiling, they become the person in the center. If they can respond without cracking even a teensy smile, then the same person remains in the center of the circle and has to try to get one of the other cowgirls to smile.

Tumbleweed Cookies

Makes 2 dozen

2 C. butterscotch chips   1 C. salted peanuts
2 C. chow mein noodles

In a double boiler over simmering water, melt the butterscotch chips, stirring frequently until smooth. Remove from heat and stir in chow mein noodles and peanuts. Drop by teaspoonfuls onto waxed paper. Refrigerate until firm.

Trail Mix Clusters

1 (12 oz.) pkg. white   1 C. dried fruit, such as
   baking chips   cranberries, raisins,
2 C. rice and corn   diced apricots
   cereal squares   ¼ C. peanuts

In a large microwave-safe bowl, heat white baking chips in microwave, stopping to stir every 30 seconds, until completely melted. Gently stir in cereal squares, dried fruit and peanuts. Mix until well coated. Drop by tablespoonfuls onto waxed paper. Refrigerate for 1 hour, until firm. Cover and store leftovers in refrigerator.

Western Mad Lib

Read the story below by filling in the blanks with the corresponding response. See what crazy tales you can come up with!

Female friend 1	_____
Female friend 2	_____
Silly name 1	_____
Silly name 2	_____
Furniture (plural)	_____
Animal 1 (singular)	_____
Animal 2 (singular)	_____
Adverb	_____
City or Town	_____
Number	_____
Animal 3 (singular)	_____

Female friend 1 and Female friend 2 had a sleepover at Female friend 1's house last weekend. Both had a lot of fun. The girls played a lot of games, but their favorite one was "Cowgirl," since they both like riding horses so much. They pretended they were cowgirls in the Old West.

They changed their names to Buckaroo Female friend 1 and Cowpoke Female friend 2, with their trusty horses, Silly name 1 and Silly name 2. They ran around the house, herding Furniture instead of cattle, yelling "Get along little doggies!" They practiced their roping skills, using belts and chasing the Animal 1 around the house. Luckily, the Animal 2 was too smart for them and hid under the couch!

Their favorite activity was singing cowgirl songs, like this one…
"Get along little Animal 2,
you move way too Adverb,
We have to get to City or Town in the north of Idaho!
We have Number head of Animal 3
to move way out West,
but you're moving too slow,
you are such a pest!"

Flip Flop Invitations

You can purchase thin foam paper from your local crafts store and cut it in the shape of a flip flop. You can attach small plastic flowers or decorations. Create the straps out of additional foam paper and attach with crafter's glue. Write the details of the party in permanent marker on the bottom of the flip flop. If you don't want to create your own flip flop, use a real one! Purchase cheap sandals from the store and write directly on those!

Palm Tree Invitations

There's nothing more tropical than palm trees. Trace the shape of a palm tree onto a brown paper bag and cut it out. Include the details of the party on the trunk of the tree. Cut palm leaves out of green paper and attach to the trunk with glue. You may want to add some coconuts hanging from the tree branches!

Mango Tango Smoothie

Makes 1 serving

1 C. mango slices
2 T. white grape juice

4 scoops vanilla ice cream
or frozen yogurt

In a blender, combine the mango slices, white grape juice and ice cream. Process on high until well blended. Pour into a tall glass and serve.

Sun Tea Punch

Makes 10 servings

6 to 8 decaffeinated
tea bags
½ gallon water
4 oranges, divided

8 lemons, divided
$\frac{1}{3}$ C. honey
½ bunch fresh mint leaves

Steep the tea bags in the water by placing out in the sun for 3 or more hours. After at least 3 hours, remove the tea bags and squeeze the juice of 3 of the oranges and 7 of the lemons into the tea. Add the honey and stir until well combined. Cut the remaining 1 orange and remaining 1 lemon into slices and stir into the tea. Pour tea into glasses and garnish each serving with a sprig of fresh mint leaves.

Hawaiian Names

Once the guests arrive at the party, challenge them each to come up with their own Hawaiian name. Address each other by these names for the rest of the party. But the catch is that the name can be made up of only the twelve letters of the Hawaiian alphabet. Those letters are a, e, h, i, k, l, m, n, o, p, u and w.

Mini Pineapple Pizzas

Makes 8 servings

½ lb. ground Italian
  sausage
½ tsp. garlic salt
¼ tsp. dried oregano
1 C. crushed pineapple,
  drained

4 English muffins, split
1 (6 oz.) can tomato paste
1 (8 oz.) pkg. shredded
  mozzarella cheese

Preheat oven to 350°. Lightly grease a medium baking sheet. In a medium skillet over medium high heat, cook the ground Italian sausage until evenly browned. Remove from heat and drain the fat from the skillet. Mix in the garlic salt, dried oregano and crushed pineapple. Arrange the English muffin halves on the greased baking sheet. Spread an even layer of tomato paste over each muffin half and spread a generous amount of the Italian sausage mixture over each muffin half. Top each mini pizza with shredded mozzarella cheese. Bake in oven for 10 to 15 minutes, or until cheese is melted and the muffins are lightly browned.

Make Your Own Grass Skirts

Have grass skirts ready for your guests to put on once they arrive or have each guest make their own during the party! You will need lengths of string long enough to tie around each guest's waist. Measure the length of "grass" that you will need for each guest by measuring the distance from their hip bone to their ankle (it may be a different length for each person).

Tear different colored streamers into that length and have everyone fold ½" of one end of the streamer over the string and secure into place with a staple or piece of tape. Repeat with the remaining streamers until skirt is full. Tie the skirts around everyone's waist and do the hula dance!

Paper Leis

It can't be a Hawaiian Party without giving everyone a flower lei to wear around their neck or head. You can either make the leis in advance or let guests make their own as they arrive. You will need a lot of straws and colorful cupcake liners. Flatten the colored liners into circles and cut the edges to look like flowers. Cut the straws into 1" pieces. To assemble the lei, string the paper flowers onto a length of string and use the pieces of straw as spacers between the flowers.

Flamingo Stance Dance

Pair the guests off in teams of two. Have each player stand facing each other and stand with their hands on each other's shoulders. The two players have to stand on one leg while wrapping their other leg around their partner's leg. The winners are the team that can keep their balance longer than the other pairs.

Hawaiian Queen

Have all but two of the players join hands to form a circle. One of the two players not in the chain must turn away from the group – she is the Hawaiian Queen. The other player must have the circle of players weave over and under each others arms and twist into a knot without the players breaking their hold together. When the group is all knotted up, the Hawaiian Queen gets to turn around and try to untangle the players by giving orders. She can tell the players to either go over or under another player's arms or legs, but she is not allowed to touch the group or point with her hands – she can only announce her orders. The purpose is to try to untangle the players until they are in their original circle again.

Flashlight Limbo

You will need two flashlights and an open space in a very dark room. Have two girls stand about 6 feet apart holding the flash lights. Have the two girls turn on the lights and shine a beam to form the limbo pole. Play limbo music as everyone tries to get under the pole. For every round, have the girls lower their beam of light by 6 inches.

Hula Contest

You will need two hula hoops. Divide the guests into two teams and have the teams face off. Have one player from each team see who can keep the hula hoop going around their waist the longest. Keep doing this until it is down to only two players (the game may have to be divided into rounds) and then have a face off with the remaining players.

Sleeping Bag Invitations

You could shape your invitations like a sleeping bag. Write all the details on a sheet of heavyweight paper. Wrap the sheet in cotton or shiny material and roll the fabric and invitation just like you would a sleeping bag. Tie into place with pieces of string or elastic. You could place this inside a small box filled with cotton. Attach the addresses and required postage to the box and send your invitations out!

Marshmallow Invitations

You could write the details of the party directly on marshmallows! Use a pen to gently write the date of the party on one marshmallow, the address on another, the time on another one, and any other details on one more marshmallow. Gather the marshmallows in a small box and tape closed. Include the postage and address on the outside of the box and send them out! The marshmallows may be stale once they arrive, so you'll want to include a note that says, "We promise we'll have fresh marshmallows at the party to make S'mores!"

Survival Kit

Every trip to the "wilderness" requires a survival kit. Make these survival kits for your guests and be sure to include a little note for the reason each item was included.

Foil	because you always find a way to "shine"!
Candle	because you always "light" up the room!
LifeSavers	may all the rest of your days be the very best ones of your "life"!
Candy	may you continue to be as "sweet" as you are!
Sprinkles	to shower you with a "rainbow" of happiness!
Crayons	so you can have a bright and "colorful" year!
Fun streamer	may your life be filled with "fun" and special dreams come true!
Pen	wishing you all the happiness a day can "hold"!
Calendar	to fill your days with lots of sweet surprises all "year" through!
Starburst	to give you a "burst" of energy when you need it!
Whoppers	because I hope you have a "whopping" good time!
Dog bone candy	because I'm "doggone" happy to have you as a guest!

Pizza Pockets

Makes 2 servings

1 T. butter, softened
4 slices white bread
¼ C. pizza sauce
12 to 18 pepperoni slices

1 (4 oz.) can sliced
mushrooms, drained
½ C. shredded
mozzarella cheese

You will need one or more pie irons, matches, non-stick cooking spray, a can opener and a hot pad. Build a flaming campfire or toast these over a kitchen gas burner (but a campfire is more fun).

Generously grease both sides of the pie iron with non-stick cooking spray. Spread butter over one side of each slice of bread. Place one slice of bread, buttered side out, into one side of the pie iron. Layer half of the pizza sauce, pepperoni slices, mushrooms and shredded mozzarella cheese onto the bread slice. Cover with another slice of bread, buttered side out. Close iron and hold over flames for 3 minutes on each side. Remove iron from fire and open carefully with a hot pad or oven mitt. Repeat with remaining ingredients.

Campfire Apple or Cherry Turnovers

Makes 4 servings

2 T. butter, softened
8 slices white bread

1 (12 oz.) can apple or
cherry pie filling

You will need one or more pie irons, matches, non-stick cooking spray, a knife, a can opener, a spoon and a hot pad. Build a flaming campfire or toast these over a kitchen gas burner (but a campfire is more fun).

Generously grease both sides of the pie iron with non-stick cooking spray. Spread butter over one side of each slice of bread. Place one slice of bread, buttered side out, into one side of the pie iron. Spoon some of the apple or cherry pie filling into the center of the bread slice. Cover with another slice of bread, buttered side out. Close iron and hold over flames for 2 to 3 minutes on each side. Remove iron from fire and open carefully with a hot pad or oven mitt. Repeat with remaining ingredients.

Donut Snakes

Makes 8 servings

1 tube of 8 refrigerated
  biscuits
1/4 C. butter, melted

2 T. sugar
1 tsp. cinnamon

You will need long pointed sticks or skewers for each person, matches, plates and a basting brush. Build a campfire or toast these over a kitchen gas burner (but a campfire is more fun).

Unroll each biscuit and shape into a long strip. Wrap each biscuit around a long clean stick or long metal skewer. Hold the sticks so the biscuits are about 6" to 10" above the hot coals. When biscuits are browned, push biscuits off sticks and onto a plate. Brush biscuits with melted butter. In a small bowl, combine the sugar and cinnamon. Sprinkle this mixture over the melted butter and enjoy!

Flashlight Tag

This is a great game for after the sun goes down. To begin, divide the players into groups of two. Each group needs to create their own secret flashlight signal, for example; one short and one long flash, or three short flashes, etc.).

The two partners must then go off in separate directions across the yard or a large open field. The players are given one minute to scatter in different directions before they can begin flashing their secret signals. The first pair to reunite as quickly as possible by recognizing their secret signal is the winner. No talking allowed!

Piggly Wiggly

Choose one person to be "it". That person has to leave the room or tent while everyone hides inside a different sleeping bag. Everyone should switch sleeping bags so the person who is "it" won't know who is in each bag.

After about 2 minutes, "it" should return to the room or tent and gently sit on one of the sleeping bags and say, "Piggly Wiggly". The person inside the bag that has been sat on then has to make an "oink oink" noise. "It" has to then make a guess at who is in the bag. If she guesses correctly, the person inside the bag is the next "it". If they guess incorrectly, then they must leave the room again and everyone hides inside a different sleeping bag for the next round.

Silhouettes

This game works well when played outside at night. Hang up a white sheet on the clothesline and have half of the guests stand or sit on one side of the sheet. Place a light on the other side of the sheet, about 10 feet back. The remaining guests go to the other side of the sheet and, one at a time, they stand between the light and the sheet. Their shadow will be cast onto the sheet for the people sitting on the other side. The object of the game is to try to guess who is standing behind the sheet by looking at only their shadow. The people standing behind the sheet can try to trick the other players by swapping clothes or "camouflaging" their shadow by holding or carrying other objects.

Marshmallow Relay

You will need one toothpick for each player and two marshmallows. Divide all the guests into two teams and have everyone stick the toothpick in their mouth, holding one end between their teeth.

The two teams have to stand in a line and try to pass the marshmallow from one person to the next using only the toothpicks in their mouths. The first team to pass their marshmallow all the way down the line is the winner!

MOVIE
STAR
NIGHT

Movie Star Invitations

Make each of your guests a famous movie star by writing their name on a cut out star – just like in Hollywood. Write the details of the party on the other side of the invitation. Add glitter and decorations to jazz it up!

Red Carpet Invitations

Roll out the red carpet for your guests by enticing them with Red Carpet Invitations. Purchase actual red carpet or red felt material and roll it around your written invitations.

Movie Ticket Invitations

Create invitations that look just like movie tickets – guests can hand these over as they enter the door (it is their ticket to get inside!). Include the party details on one side and the words "Admit One" on the other.

Who Am I?

Write the names of famous Movie Stars on index cards and tape one to the back of each guest as they enter the party. Make sure the guest doesn't see the name written on their card – they are not supposed to know who they are! Have each guest talk to each other as if they were the person on the card by asking about famous things they've done, or songs they've written or movies they have starred in, but be sure to instruct everyone not to use that person's name. Throughout the party, as people correctly guess who they are supposed to be, have them continue to treat each other with the fake identities until everyone has guessed correctly.

Name That Star

Write the names of well-known singers and movie stars on pieces of paper. Have your guests take turns drawing the slips of paper. Have each person either sing a verse of one of the famous singer's songs, or mimic the actor or actress in a famous role. Everyone else has to try to correctly guess the star. You can award prizes for the best performances.

Movie Night Popcorn

Make individual bags of microwave popcorn and mix with the following combinations.

Double Cheddar Popcorn

Mix 2 tablespoons melted butter with 2 tablespoons of dry macaroni and cheese topping. Pour over popped popcorn and toss until well combined. If desired, mix in 2 cups Cheddar snack crackers or salsa flavored snack crackers.

Peanut Butter & Jelly Popcorn

Mix 2 tablespoons melted butter with 1 tablespoon grape or strawberry flavored drink mix powder. Pour over popped popcorn and toss until well combined. If desired, mix in 2 cups miniature Nutter Butter sandwich cookies.

Hodge Podge Popcorn

Mix 2 tablespoons melted butter with ¼ cup grated Parmesan cheese. Pour over popped popcorn and toss until well combined. If desired, mix in 1 cup Ritz Bits cheese crackers, 1 cup cocktail peanuts and ½ cup raisins.

Sugar & Spice Popcorn

Mix 2 tablespoons melted butter with 1 tablespoon sugar and ½ teaspoon cinnamon. Pour over popped popcorn and toss until well combined. If desired, mix in 1 cup honey roasted peanuts and 1 cup teddy bear cinnamon graham crackers.

Make Your Own Film

You can have lots of fun planning, writing and starring in your own films, commercials or music videos. Have all your guests plan and write the script together and assemble the necessary materials. Have a parent or someone in the group tape the film with a video recorder.

You might want to designate everyone to have certain roles, such as director, actresses, sound person, wardrobe, back up singers, etc. Make sure to play the tape for everyone once the filming is done. This is sure to bring lots of laughs and you'll always have something to remind you of your great party!

Awards Ceremony

This is a fun activity and celebration to honor the special things about each guest at the party. You could even ask everyone to bring fancy dresses to wear as if they were going to an actual awards night ceremony.

Before getting dressed up, have everyone decorate a piece of paper for the other guests at the party, so everyone will be creating one certificate for every other guest except for themselves. The awards can be serious (something they think is great about that person), or silly things like "Best Sleeper – the award for the person who snores the loudest!" Provide markers and crayons so the awarder can decorate her certificates to hand out.

Before the awards ceremony begins, serve fancy appetizers or decorate the home with balloons or candles. If you can, roll out a red carpet for each guest to walk down as they enter the party. Add an extra touch by playing music softly in the background. During the awards ceremony, each person gets to stand and be recognized as the other guests present their certificates and explain why they are giving it to that person. Encourage everyone to give silly Thank You speeches for their awards.

Dip for the Stars

Makes about 30 servings

1 C. butter, softened
¾ lb. crumbled feta cheese
1 (8 oz.) pkg. cream
  cheese, softened
2 cloves garlic, minced
1 shallot, minced
3 T. ginger ale

Ground white pepper,
  to taste
½ C. pine nuts, toasted*
1 C. chopped sun-dried
  tomatoes
¾ C. pesto sauce

In a blender or food processor, combine butter, feta cheese, cream cheese, minced garlic, minced shallot, ginger ale and white pepper. Blend until smooth. Grease a medium bowl or gelatin mold and line with plastic wrap for easy removal. On the bottom, layer half of the sun-dried tomatoes, half of the pine nuts, half of the pesto and half of the cheese mixture, in that order. Repeat layers and pat down. Refrigerate at least 1 hour. Turn the dip out onto a serving plate and remove plastic wrap. Serve with an assortment of crackers, vegetables and chips for dipping.

* To toast, place pine nuts in a single layer on a baking sheet. Bake at 350° for approximately 10 minutes or until pine nuts are golden brown.

Movie Trivia

Before everyone comes over, have a sibling or parent watch the movie that you are going to show. Ask them to write down trivia questions about things that happen in the movie. Show the movie during your party and warn everyone to be very observant. Once the movie is over, have someone read the trivia questions to each player. If the player can't answer their question, they can pass their turn to the next player. The player with the most correct answers is the winner!

Some trivia questions about the movie could be related to what a certain actor or actress was wearing in one of the scenes, what city or state the movie takes place in, who can recite a famous line from the movie, etc. Make sure there are plenty of questions for everyone and try to be tricky! Your guests may even want you to play back a part of the movie so they can see a detail they might have missed.

Pennant Flag Invitations

Make invitations that look like pennant flags for different sport teams, schools or universities. Use the design below to make a template for your invitations, or make a bigger one out of construction paper. Write the details of the party on one side of the pennant. You could even cover the front side of the invitation with letters and designs cut out of felt.

Sports Ticket Invitations

Create invitations that look just like tickets to a sporting event – guests can hand those over as they enter the door (it is their ticket to get inside!). Include the date, time and address on one side of the ticket, arranging these to look like the details of a sporting event on a real ticket. Write additional party details on the other side.

Concession Stand

A fun thing to do for a sports themed party would be to create your own concession stand that guests can order food from throughout the evening. You could set up a table or turn the kitchen into the concession area by designating a doorway as the place to order the food.

Gather fun containers, such as popcorn buckets, cardboard hot dog cartons, cups and straws for soda, or square paper plates for nachos. Write out the food options and prices on a chalkboard or white board. When everyone arrives, they could be given fake money or tickets that they can redeem for snacks at the concession stand. Ask a parent or sibling to work in the concession stand. This is guaranteed to be a big hit!

Ultimate Frisbee

You will need a large open space, at least four players and one Frisbee. Divide the open space into the playing field by designating two end zones at either end of the field. A regulation field is 40 yards x 70 yards, with end zones that are 25 yards deep.

Divide all players into two even teams. In each round of play, one team acts as the offense and the opposing team acts as the defense. At the start of each round, both teams begin by lining up inside their respective end zones. The team that is on defense throws the Frisbee towards the team on offense. The team on offense catches the Frisbee and tries to pass it down the field toward the other team's end zone. If they reach the end zone, the team scores 1 point. The rules are as follows:

- The Frisbee can be thrown in any direction.
- When a player has the Frisbee, they may not run, but are allowed only 2 steps before they have to throw the Frisbee again. This person has only 10 seconds to throw the Frisbee before it is turned over to the opposing team.
- The Frisbee changes possession when a pass is not completed or is intercepted by a player on the opposing team. The Frisbee also changes possession when it is thrown out of bounds, dropped, blocked or if the thrower takes more than 2 steps or holds the Frisbee for more than 10 seconds.
- The first team to score 21 points wins.

Make Your Own Pennant Flags

You could have all your guests make pennant flags at the party as a favor to take home, or make them in advance to decorate the house or a certain room.

You will need large pieces of felt in different colors, fabric glue, scissors and a long piece of string. Cut the fabric into long wedges that are 10" to 12" at the wide end. Cut the other end to a point. Cut letters or emblems out of different colored felt and glue them to one side of the pennant. Hang the pennants on the string by folding the top 1" of fabric over the string and gluing into place with more fabric glue. You could make one pennant flag with the name of each guest and let that guest take their flag home with them at the end of the party.

You Said It!

You will need one clothespin for each player. At the beginning of the party, clip 1 clothespin onto the shirt of each person. Warn each player that if another player hears them say the words "tired", "sports" or "party", that player has the right to take the faulty player's clothespin away. The winner is the person who has collected the most clothespins by the end of the party. Any words can be chosen to be the "forbidden words". Make the game more difficult by designating the forbidden words as the names of guests.

Blind Man Ball Game

You will need two big baskets, 6 balls of any kind and 2 handkerchiefs. Separate the players into two even teams. Each team will have 1 basket filled with 3 balls and 1 handkerchief. Place the baskets of balls 6 feet in front of each team. Blindfold the first player of each team with the handkerchief and dump the balls from the baskets. The blindfolded players will have to retrieve 3 balls each and return them to her team's basket before passing the handkerchief to the next player. The non-blindfolded players can help their blindfolded teammate by giving her only verbal directions. The blindfolded player can retrieve any three balls (even the ones from the other team) but they must be returned to her team's basket. If she puts the ball(s) in the wrong basket, they will count for the other team. Once the blindfolded player has put 3 balls in her team's basket, the next player is blindfolded and the balls are dumped from the basket. The winning team is the first to complete one rotation of players.

Strike Three!

All you will need is a deck of cards. If there are more than 4 players, use two decks of cards. Shuffle the cards and deal them, face down, in front of each player so that everyone has the same amount of cards.

To play, each person has to take the top card in the pile and immediately turn it face up in the center pile. When anyone plays a winning card (Ace, King, Queen or Jack), everyone has to perform the required action for that card. The purpose of the game is to try to be the first person to perform each action. That person gets to keep all the cards. The person with the most cards at the end of the game is the winner. A lot of the fun comes from deciding who actually performed the action first. If more than one of the winning cards are laid down in the same turn, then the Ace takes priority, followed by the King, then Queen and finally the Jack. If there are none of these cards played in the round, the cards are pushed aside and no one gets to take them. These cards should be re-shuffled into the deck for the next game.

Ace: If someone lays an Ace face up on the table, everyone has to slap their palm down on top of it. The person whose hand is at the bottom of the pile gets to keep all the cards for that round.

King: Everyone has to perform a British army salute by putting their right hand up to their forehead. The first person to do this gets to keep all the cards for that round.

Queen: Everyone has to yell out "Strike Three! You're Out!" at the top of their voices. The first person to do this gets to keep all the cards for that round.

Jack: Everyone has to raise their hand as if they were in class as fast as they can. The first person to do this gets to keep all the cards for that round.

Double Dressing

You will need at least six people for this game and a pair of dice. Collect different sports clothing and gear, such as a catcher's face mask and pads, a football helmet, sports bra, a jersey, soccer cleats, football shoulder pads, pom poms, etc. Ensure that all of the clothing and gear are large enough to fit any of the guests.

To play, arrange all of your guests to sit in a circle and place all of the sports clothing and gear in a large pile in the center of the circle. One person begins by rolling the pair of dice. This person rolls once and then the person to the right has to roll the dice. This continues as people roll dice around the circle until someone rolls a double (the two dice both have the same number).

When someone does roll a double, everyone shouts "Doubles!" and that person has to begin dressing themselves with all of the equipment in the center pile. The person continues dressing, trying to put on as much clothing and equipment as possible, until someone else rolls a double. If this happens while the person in the middle is dressing, that person has to immediately begin taking off the sports clothing and gear and the new person puts it on. The object of the game is for the person in the middle to put on all of the sports equipment before someone else rolls a double. If one of the players can achieve this, with all of the clothing on their body in any fashion, then that person is the winner.

Mardi Gras

Mask Invitations

Create invitations in the shape of Mardi Gras masks. Use heavyweight paper to cut out a mask shape, or use the template on page 74. Decorate one side of each mask with sequins and glitter and write the details of the party on the other side. Make the masks an appropriate size to slip inside the envelopes.

Mardi Gras Invitations

The traditional colors of Mardi Gras are purple, green and gold. Use these colors to decorate your invitations. The color Purple represents Justice, the color Green represents Faith and the color Gold stands for Power.

Lots & Lots o' Beads

It just can't be Mardi Gras without having lots of beads! Give a string of beads to guests as they enter the party, as favors to take home or just string around the house for decoration!

You will need lots of medium to large sized beads with holes and lengths of string. Separate the beads by color – empty egg cartons work nicely to keep the beads separated. Give each guest a length of string and let them string the beads of their choice onto the string. Tie the ends together to form a necklace. Have plenty of beads so all guests can make lots of necklaces to wear throughout the evening!

History of Mardi Gras

Share some Mardi Gras history with your guests.

The New Orleans celebration of Mardi Gras began in 1837, which also marked the year of the first street parade. Mardi Gras actually lasts for an entire season and always starts on January 6th, twelve days after Christmas. During the Mardi Gras season, there are many celebrations and masked balls to attend. One of the biggest festivities is the Mardi Gras parade, including large extravagant floats. The crew members on the floats throw beads and other items to the people lining the streets. Marching bands and people wearing purple, green and gold costumes also join in the parades. The carnival season ends on Mardi Gras day (also known as Fat Tuesday), which is always 46 days before Easter. Many of the largest parades and celebrations are held on this day.

Original King Cake

½ C. warm water
(110° to 115°F)

2 (1 oz.) pkgs. active
dry yeast

½ C. plus 2 tsp. sugar,
divided

3½ C. flour

1 tsp. nutmeg

2 tsp. salt

1 tsp. grated lemon peel

½ C. warm milk

5 egg yolks

½ C. plus 2 T. butter,
divided

1 tsp. cinnamon

1 (1˝) small plastic baby
or toy

Place the warm water in a small shallow bowl and sprinkle with the yeast and 2 teaspoons sugar. Set aside for 3 minutes before thoroughly mixing. After mixing, set the bowl aside for about 10 minutes, or until the yeast bubbles up and the mixture almost doubles in volume. Into a large mixing bowl, sift the flour, remaining ½ cup sugar, nutmeg and salt. Stir in the lemon peel and form a well in the center of the mixture. Pour the yeast mixture and warm milk into the hole. Add egg yolks and stir slowly with a wooden spoon. When the mixture is smooth, beat in ½ cup butter, 1 tablespoon at a time. Continue to beat for 2 minutes, or until the dough can be formed into a soft ball. Knead the dough on a lightly floured surface, sprinkling with additional flour until dough is no longer sticky. Knead the dough for 10 minutes, until shiny and elastic. Coat the inside of a large bowl with 1 tablespoon butter and place the dough in the bowl, rotating dough to cover it with the butter. Cover the bowl with a kitchen towel and set aside for 1½ hours, or until the dough doubles in volume. Grease a large baking sheet with the additional 1 tablespoon butter. Remove dough from bowl and punch down. Sprinkle with cinnamon and shape dough into a cylinder. Twist the cylinder and shape the dough into a loop, pinching the ends together to seal.

(recipe continued on next page)

(recipe continued from previous page)

Place on baking sheet. Cover dough with a towel and set aside for 45 minutes, or until dough doubles in volume. Preheat oven to 375°. If desired, you can place the plastic baby doll or toy in the unbaked cake at this time. Bake in oven for 25 to 35 minutes. Remove cake from oven and let cool. Once cooled, spread white icing over top and sides of cake. Sprinkle green, purple and gold colored sugar over the icing. Tradition says that the person who receives the piece of cake with the plastic toy has to throw the next party!

Shrimp Artichoke Dip

Makes 32 servings

1 C. shredded
  Cheddar cheese
1 C. grated
  Parmesan cheese
1 (14 oz.) can artichoke
  hearts, drained
½ C. chopped green
  onions

½ tsp. garlic salt
½ C. mayonnaise
1 C. cooked and
  peeled shrimp
Paprika, optional

Preheat oven to 350°. In a small to medium baking dish, combine shredded Cheddar cheese, grated Parmesan cheese, drained artichoke hearts, chopped green onions, garlic salt, mayonnaise and peeled shrimp. Mix until well combined. Sprinkle paprika over top. Bake in oven for 20 minutes, or until top of dip is bubbly and lightly browned. Serve with tortilla chips, crackers or fresh cut vegetables for dipping.

Louisiana Seafood Boil

Makes 16 servings

Water
4 bags Crab Boil mix
4 lbs. whole new potatoes
16 pieces short ear corn
2 lbs. link sausages,
   precooked

2 lbs. shrimp, shelled
   and deveined
2 lbs. crawfish

Fill a turkey fryer pot halfway with water. Set fryer to medium-high setting and bring water to a boil. It should take about 10 minutes to heat the water. Add Crab Boil mix bags. When water is boiling, add the potatoes. After potatoes have been in boiling water for 6 minutes, add the ears of corn. After 3 minutes, add precooked sausage links. After an additional 3 minutes, add shrimp and crawfish. Total cook time should be about 27 minutes. To serve, cover a picnic table with thick paper or newspaper. Remove fryer basket from turkey fryer and let ingredients drain of water. Pour entire basket of food onto newspaper in the middle of the table and encourage everyone to eat right from the table – Louisiana style!

Mardi Gras Masks

You will need heavyweight paper, a paper punch, lengths of string or yarn, markers, glue, glitter, sequins and bright colored feathers. Photocopy or cut out and trace the template on the next page onto heavy weight paper for each guest. When each guest arrives, have them cut out the mask from the paper. Using a paper punch, make a hole in either side of the mask where indicated. Encourage guests to decorate their own masks with markers, glitter, sequins and feathers – the more extravagant the better! Complete the Mardi Gras theme by having everyone wear their masks throughout the evening.

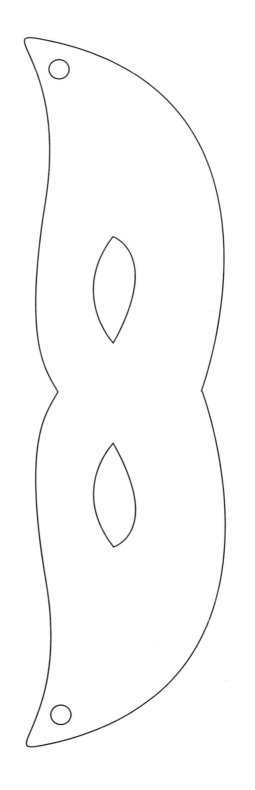

Tombstone Invitations

Cut your invitations in a tombstone shape out of gray textured paper, or use heavyweight white paper and spray with faux stone spray paint. Write all the details on the invitation with a black marker. You might want to encourage everyone to dress in scary costumes!

Spider Web Invitations

Create spider web paper by placing a sheet of black paper snuggly inside a cake pan (a 5 x 9" loaf pan works well). Squirt a little white paint in the middle of the paper and place a marble in the pan. Swirl the pan back and forth so the marble makes a white design on the black paper. Let the paper dry and write the details of the party on the other side of the paper using a silver or white gel pen. You could even glue a few small plastic spiders on the web!

Putrid Punch

Makes 14 servings

1 (13 oz.) pkg. lemon
   lime drink mix
1 C. sugar
8 C. water
1 (12 oz.) can frozen
   orange juice concentrate

4 C. ginger ale
3 scoops orange sherbet
Gummy worms

In a large punch bowl, combine lemon lime drink mix, sugar and water. Stir until sugar and drink mix are completely dissolved. Stir in the orange juice concentrate. Before serving, stir in the ginger ale, orange sherbet and gummy worms. The punch will have a disgusting color, but surprisingly tastes great!

Note: To make the gummy worms float, you could add gummy worms to ice cube trays and fill with water. Place in freezer until gummy worm cubes are frozen and add to punch before serving.

Graveyard Mud Cookies

Makes about 3 dozen

2 C. sugar
¼ tsp. butter
½ C. milk
3 T. cocoa powder
1 tsp. vanilla

5 C. quick cooking oats, divided
½ C. crunchy peanut butter

In a double boiler over medium high heat, combine sugar, butter, milk and cocoa powder. Bring mixture to a boil, stirring often. Let boil for 1 minute and remove from heat. Stir in vanilla, 3 cups oats and crunchy peanut butter. Slowly add additional 2 cups oats until desired consistency is reached. Quickly drop mixture by heaping teaspoonfuls onto waxed paper. Chill in refrigerator until hardened.

Worms on a Bun

Makes 4 servings

4 hot dogs   Ketchup
4 hamburger bun halves

Cut each hot dog lengthwise into five or six long strips. Fill a medium pot halfway with water and bring to a boil over medium high heat. Add hot dog strips to water and heat until the hot dog pieces curl up like wiggly worms. Remove the "worms" from water and let drain. Pile the worms up on each hamburger bun half and drizzle with ketchup.

Mr. Kreepy

Scare all your guests by passing around the body parts of the deceased Mr. Kreepy, your frightening old neighbor!

You will need 8 containers to hold the assorted slimy-feeling foods that you will pass around. Fill one container with a thick slice of bologna and place a big chunk of ham and water in a bowl. Place a canned pear half on a plate and cooked ramen noodles that have been rinsed in cold water on another plate. Place two peeled grapes in a small bowl. Place a large head of broccoli in a bowl and sprinkle prepared gelatin over top. Cut small pickle spears in half and place them in a bowl. In the last container, place five frozen French fries with one slivered almond stuck to the end of each one. Once the guests arrive, have them sit in a circle. Turn off the lights and pass the containers of food around, encouraging each guest to feel the "body part" as you read this tale… "We once had an old neighbor named Mr. Kreepy. Sad old fellow. He often complained about not feeling quite right. When he died last month, he donated his body to science, hoping that researchers could learn new things from his story. Perhaps you can help with the diagnosis…"

"Was his problem an oversized tongue?" Pass the container with the thick slice of bologna

"Or a heart that never beat quite right?" Pass around the chunk of ham in water

"An unusually small stomach?" Pass around the canned halved pear

"Maybe it was his thick, cold veins?" Pass around the cold cooked ramen noodles

"Or his defective eyeballs?" Pass around the peeled grapes

"Perhaps it was his genius-sized brain?" Pass around the cauliflower with prepared gelatin

"Could it be his long, knobby toes?" Pass around the halved pickle spears

"Or his ice-cold fingers with dry, brittle nails?" Pass around the frozen French fries and slivered almonds

Scary Noises

To play this game, choose one of the guests to be "it". Everyone else has to sit in a circle around the person who is "it". Place a blindfold around "it's" eyes so she can't see. "It" has to count to ten while everyone else in the circle scrambles into a different order around the circle, so the person in the middle won't know who is where. Then "it" has to stick out their hand and point at one person. That person has to make a scary noise (a grunt, squeak, ooh, ahh, growl, etc.). Then, "it" has to guess the name of the person who made the noise. If they guess correctly, the person who made the noise becomes "it". If they guess incorrectly, the game starts over and everyone shuffles around again. "It" points at a new person who has to make a scary noise.

The Mummy Game

Split your guests into teams of 3 and give each team one extra thick roll of toilet paper. You will need a stopwatch. Have each team choose one person to be the mummy. The other two team members wrap the third member in the toilet roll so they look like an Egyptian mummy. The winning team is the one who has the neatest and most covered mummy after 2 minutes.

Squeeze Murder

Before everyone arrives, gather enough little slips of paper to have one for every person. Write the letter "M" on one of the slips of paper, keeping all the other papers blank. Crumple up the papers and place them in an empty dish.

To start the game, have all of your guests sit in a circle. Everyone has to draw one slip of paper, keeping it out of sight of the other players. The person who gets the "M" is the Murderer, but they have to keep it a secret. Now, turn out the lights and have everyone join hands in the circle. The Murderer has to choose someone else in the circle to "kill". They count how many people are between themselves and the victim and then give the hand next to them that many "squeezes". For example, if the Murderer is sitting 3 people away from the person they choose to kill, they would squeeze the hand next to them 3 times. Then that person would squeeze the hand next to them 2 times, the next person would squeeze the hand next to them 1 time. The person whose hand is squeezed only once has to perform an outlandish, exaggerated death. Turn the lights back on and the "dead" person gets to choose who their Murderer was. If they guess correctly, the victim gets a prize. If they guess incorrectly, the Murderer gets a prize. To strategize, the Murderer will want to wait a few moments after the lights go out before squeezing the hand next to them.

Rock & Roll Party

CD Invitations

You could send real CDs as your invitations. Use old CDs or purchase a pack of recordable CDs at your local store. Write the details of the party on one side of the CD in permanent marker. Make sure to let the ink dry so it won't smudge. You could also cover the CD in black paper to make it look more like a record, or create your own CD label using sticky paper. There are many label-making programs available. You could send your CD invitations in a real CD case – just tape the case closed and stick the address label and postage right on the case!

Guitar Invitations

Create invitations in the shape of the most famous rock and roll instrument – the guitar! Cut your desired guitar shape out of crazy patterned paper. You could use real pieces of string or thread as the guitar strings. Hold them into place with brads or eyelets. Write the details of the party on one side of the guitar. Slip the mini guitars inside envelopes and send 'em out to get the neighborhood excited about your upcoming rockin' party!

Chocolate Milk Shakes

Makes 5 (1 cup) servings

3 C. milk, chilled
1 (4 oz.) pkg. instant
   chocolate pudding mix

3 scoops vanilla ice cream
Whipped topping, optional

In a blender, combine the cold milk, instant chocolate pudding mix and vanilla ice cream. Process on high for 15 seconds or until well blended. Pour milk shakes into five cups and, if desired, top each one with a dollop of whipped topping.

Old Fashioned Vanilla Malt

Makes 1 serving

½ C. milk, chilled
¼ C. carbonated water
3 T. malted milk powder

½ tsp. vanilla
2 scoops vanilla ice cream

In a blender, combine cold milk, carbonated water, malted milk powder and vanilla. Add vanilla ice cream and process on high until well blended. Pour malt into a tall glass and serve.

Elvis' Favorite Sandwich

Makes 1 serving

2 T. creamy peanut butter   2 T. butter or margarine
2 slices white bread
½ very ripe banana,
  peeled

Spread peanut butter over one slice of bread. Cut the banana into slices and place them over the peanut butter. Top with the other slice of bread to form a sandwich. In a medium skillet over medium heat, melt the butter. Place the sandwich in the skillet and heat until lightly toasted on both sides, turning once.

Note: Legend says the king himself used to eat this sandwich with a knife and fork!

Root Beer Floats

Makes 2 servings

½ pint vanilla ice cream
1 (12 oz.) can or bottle
root beer

½ C. whipped cream
4 maraschino cherries

Place 1 scoop of vanilla ice cream in each of two tall glasses. Pour half of the root beer carefully over the ice cream in each glass. Add another scoop to each glass and the remaining root beer. If the glasses are not foaming over, you may add another scoop of ice cream to each. Garnish with a dollop of whipped cream and two maraschino cherries in each serving.

Purple Cow:
Replace the root beer in the above recipe with grape soda.

Pink Cow:
Replace the root beer in the above recipe with cherry or strawberry soda.

Green Cow:
Replace the root beer in the above recipe with lemon lime soda.

Brown Cow:
Replace the root beer in the above recipe with cola.

The Best Burgers

Makes 10 servings

1 sweet onion, chopped
1 green bell pepper,
 chopped
4 cloves garlic, peeled
 and crushed

1 tomato, chopped
2 T. steak sauce
2 lbs. ground beef
¼ C. dry bread crumbs
Salt and pepper to taste

Preheat a grill to high heat and lightly oil the grate. In a blender or food processor, combine chopped onion, chopped green pepper, crushed garlic and chopped tomato. Blend into a thick liquid. Stir in the steak sauce. Transfer the blended mixture to a large bowl and add ground beef. Mix until well combined and set aside for 15 minutes to allow the flavors to blend. Slowly mix in dry bread crumbs until well incorporated. Season with salt and pepper and form mixture into hamburger patties. Cook burgers on the preheated grill to desired doneness.

Skating Rink

Have all of your guests bring over a pair of roller skates so you can have a skating party. You'll want to include a line on your invitations reminding your guests not to forget their roller skates or roller blades.

Turn the driveway or garage into a roller skating rink by clearing the concrete area as the rink. You could even set up a snack bar area where your guests can order malts, milk shakes, root beer floats, burgers and fries. Ask a parent or sibling to work in the snack bar area during your party.

Decorate the area with strings of white lights and hang CDs or old records from the ceiling of the garage. Be sure to have a stereo and lots of music to play. You could even play some games like Red Rover, Red Rover or the Hokey Pokey.

Party Dice

Turn old square boxes into a pair of jumbo dice. Tape the boxes securely shut and paint the dice white (or any color that you choose). Once the paint has dried, use a large permanent marker to write these six verbs on one die:

Run
Skip
Jump
Roll
Twist
Dance

On the other die, write these six adverbs and nouns:

Quickly
Slowly
Fast
High
Low
All Around

Take turns rolling the dice. Each person has to perform the action that is listed on the top of the two dice they roll. Use can change the words on the dice to better suit your party or guests. Have fun coming up with crazy combinations.

Beach Towel Invitations

Make invitations out of comfy beach towel material by either cutting pieces from an old beach towel or buying terry cloth fabric from your local fabric or crafts store. Write the details on a piece of heavyweight paper and roll it up inside the fabric.

Seashell Invitations

Gather real seashells to make your invitations – clam shells work nicely. Use a thin-tip marker to write the invitation details right on the shell, or write the invitation on a piece of homemade paper, roll it up and stick it inside the shell.

Surfboard Invitations

Create invitations that look like miniature surfboards. Cut an 8" surfboard shape out of Fome-Cor or cardboard. Trace the shape onto colorful or patterned con-tact paper. Peel the backing off the con-tact paper and stick it to the Fome-Cor pieces. Use a black marker to write the details of the party on one side of each surfboard. Write the words "Surfs Up!" on the other side of the surfboards. Stick the miniature boards inside envelopes and send 'em out in the mail!

Beach Cake

Decorate a 9 x 13" sheet cake to look just like a beach scene. You will need one prepared cake, 2½ cups blue frosting, ¼ cup white frosting and 1 cup graham cracker crumbs. Transfer the baked cake to a flat platter. Spread the white frosting over one short end of the cake and a little more than half way over cake surface. Spread the blue frosting in a wavy line to represent the edge of the water. Use additional blue frosting to build up waves in the blue "water" side of the cake. Spread the white frosting over the remaining short end of the cake and up to the water edge. Sprinkle the graham cracker crumbs over the white frosting to look like sand.

Decorate with candy rocks to look like stones on the beach. Cut fruit striped gum into surfboard shapes and place them on the water. Add LifeSavers candies to look like inner tubes. Cut tape gum into 1" lengths and place on the sand as beach towels. Decorate with drink umbrellas as parasols. If desired, add little plastic palm trees, gummy fish, and plastic figures as people on the beach – let your imagination go wild!

Hang Ten Photos

A fun icebreaker for when everyone arrives can be to designate an area where everyone has to strike a dramatic surfing pose while their picture is taken.

To set the stage, play some Beach Boys tunes on the stereo and spread a blue tarp or blanket on the floor, representing the water of the ocean. Place a folded up ironing board on the water. Have your guests take turns "riding the waves" while you snap Polaroid photos of each of them. Hang the photos up so everyone can laugh at them throughout the party. Give each photo to that guest to take home as a souvenir!

Fruit Smoothies

Makes 4 servings

1 kiwi, peeled and sliced
1 banana, peeled
and chopped
½ C. blueberries
1 C. strawberries

1 C. ice cubes
½ C. orange juice
1 (8 oz.) container
peach yogurt

In a blender, combine the sliced kiwi, chopped banana, blueberries, strawberries, ice cubes, orange juice and peach yogurt. Process on high until blended and smooth. Divide smoothies into four cups and serve.

Beach Kabobs

Cut pieces of fruit, cheese and meat and slide them onto bamboo skewers. Use ingredients like pineapple chunks, whole strawberries, mango or papaya pieces, banana slices, grapes, Cheddar cheese cubes, Swiss cheese cubes, Colby Jack cheese cubes, smoked turkey cubes and ham cubes. These make a light and colorful treat – perfect for the beach!

Ocean Cups

Makes 4 servings

1 C. boiling water
1 (3 oz.) pkg. blue
    gelatin, any flavor
1 C. cold water

2 (1 oz.) pkgs. fish-
    shaped fruit snacks
Thawed whipped
    topping

In a medium bowl, combine boiling water and blue gelatin, mixing until completely dissolved. Stir in cold water. Pour gelatin into 4 clear plastic cups, filling about half full. Refrigerate filled glasses for about 1 hour, or until just slightly firm. Press a few fish-shape fruit snacks into each cup and return to refrigerator for an additional 3 hours. To serve, spread a little whipped topping over gelatin in each cup to look like waves.

Super Sunglasses

Purchase cheap pairs of sunglasses for each of your party guests. Gather fun decorations that everyone can use to decorate their glasses, such as little beads, sequins, fake jewels, feathers, etc. Be sure to have a hot glue gun handy so everyone can attach the decorations to their flashy super sunglasses. Encourage everyone to wear their sunglasses that night so you'll feel just like you're on a sunny beach. Let everyone take their new glasses home with them as a favor!

Fishin' Cupcakes

Makes 24 servings

24 paper cupcake liners
1 (17¾ oz.) pkg. devil's
  food cake mix
1 (16 oz.) tub
  vanilla frosting

Blue food coloring
24 cocktail straws
24 pieces dental floss
24 fish shaped fruit snacks

Prepare and bake the cake mix according to package directions for cupcakes. Remove from oven and let cupcakes cool completely. In a small bowl, combine the vanilla frosting and a few drops of blue food coloring. Spread the frosting over the cooled cupcakes, pulling up on the frosting to create "waves". Cut each straw to 3" and cut the dental floss into 3½" lengths. Attach one piece of dental floss to the end of each straw and stick one of these "fishing poles" in each cupcake. Wrap the other end of dental floss on each pole around one fish shaped fruit snack and rest the "fish" in the "water".

Indoor Beach Party

If you don't live near the ocean or a beach, that doesn't mean you can't have a Beach Party! Create that fun-in-the-sun summer feeling right inside your own home!

Spread beach towels out on the living room floor. Tell your guests to bring their swimsuits and flip flops. Sip on smoothies and feast on nachos or hot dogs. You could even make castles out of clay or play dough, or fill small plastic pools with water or sand. Be sure to put plastic down so your parents don't get angry when you spill water and sand everywhere. Wear sunglasses and beach hats – you could even spread sunscreen on your noses and give one person a whistle so they can be the lifeguard! Inflate floaties and inner tubes that everyone can lay on. Have your camera ready because you'll want to take pictures of your Indoor Beach Party!

Smiley Face Invitations

The big, round, yellow smiley face is a symbol of the carefree 70's. It reminded people to just "be happy!" Encourage your guests to get in the mood by sending out yellow smiley face invitations. Cut circles out of yellow construction paper and draw a smiley face on one side. Write the details of the party on the other side.

70's Invitations

Use other symbols of the 1970's to put on your invitations, like colorful flowers, daisies, peace signs, John Lennon and the Beatles. Purchase tie-died paper to create your invitations and include phrases like "Flower Power", "Peace" and "Have a Nice Day!" all over them.

Peace, Love & Happiness

You will need one soft "cushy" ball and at least three players. Designate one player as the first "thrower". Give all remaining players a different number. All remaining players cluster around the thrower. The thrower tosses the ball up in the air and yells, "Peace, Love and Happiness" followed by a number of one of the players.

The player whose number is called has to catch the ball while all remaining players (including the thrower) scatter in all directions. As soon as the player catches the ball, he or she has to yell, "Peace!" All remaining players have to freeze where they are. Then the player with the ball can take 3 steps in any direction. The player then tries to throw the ball at any of the other players. If the player hits another player, the hit player gets a "P". If the player throwing the ball misses another player, the throwing player gets a "P". The process goes again until one player has enough letters to spell "PEACE". When any player has all five letters, they are out. The last person remaining is the winner!

Funky Straw Art

You will need heavyweight paper and bright colored India ink. Give each guest one sheet of paper, a straw and an eye dropper. Have each guest drop different colors of the India ink onto their paper using the eye dropper. Then, each person needs to blow on the paper through the straw to spread the ink around in different patterns. This works best if one drop of ink is placed on the paper at a time and blown on with the straw before adding the next ink color. These can turn out very psychedelic!

Rainbow Ice Cream

Makes about 16 servings

½ gallon vanilla ice cream, softened

4 (3 oz.) boxes flavored gelatin mix, in four different flavors

Set the ice cream out at room temperature for 20 to 30 minutes to soften. Sprinkle about 3 tablespoons of one of the gelatin flavors over the bottom of a medium-sized square or rectangular container. Layer ¼ of the softened ice cream over the gelatin powder. Don't worry if the ice cream is lumpy or uneven – it will give the ice cream a cool effect. Next scatter about 3 tablespoons of a different gelatin flavor over the ice cream and top with another ¼ of the softened ice cream. Repeat layers with the remaining two gelatin flavors and remaining ice cream, topping the ice cream with a final layer of gelatin. Cover the container and place in freezer for about 2 to 3 hours, or until hardened. To serve, transfer the entire block of ice cream to a serving tray by running warm water over the bottom of the pan to release the ice cream. To get a nice rainbow-colored scoop, scrape the ice cream from the side of the block into individual bowls.

Psychedelic Party Mix

Makes about 18 servings

1 C. Cheerios
1 C. Corn or Rice Chex
1 C. pretzel sticks
1 C. salted or dry
   roasted peanuts

1 (14 oz.) bag M&M's
   baking bits
1 (12 oz.) bag vanilla
   baking chips
1 T. vegetable oil

In a large bowl, combine Cheerios, Chex cereal, pretzel sticks, peanuts and M&M's baking bits. Toss all together until well combined. In a double boiler over simmering water, place the vanilla baking chips. Heat, stirring often, until vanilla chips are completely melted. Fold the vegetable oil into the melted vanilla chips. Pour melted mixture over dry ingredients in bowl and toss until evenly coated. Dump mixture out onto a baking sheet lined with waxed paper and spread out to cover baking sheet. Place in refrigerator until hardened. Break into pieces and serve.

Tie Dye

Have all of your guests create their own tie-dyed clothing to take home from your 70's slumber party! You will need water, different colors of dye and rubber bands. Write on the invitations that everyone will need to bring one piece of white cotton clothing, such as T-shirts, shorts, tank tops, socks, etc. to tie dye at your party!

Fill large pots with water and add dye according to package directions. You can mix many dye colors from yellow, fuchsia and turquoise dye according to the chart below. Wrap rubber bands tightly around the white clothing. Wherever the rubber bands are placed, there will be a white marking on the clothing. Submerge the clothing pieces in the dyed water, pushing down with long tongs or a stick. You may want to wear rubber gloves so your hands and arms don't get covered in dye! Let the clothing sit in the dye for at least 15 to 20 minutes. The longer the clothing remains in the dye, the darker the color will become. Remove each clothing piece from the dye and rinse under cool water, according to dye package directions. Ring out garments until water runs clear. Carefully remove rubber bands by using a scissors to cut them from the dye garments. Let dyed garments dry completely overnight.

Yellow, Fuchsia and Turquoise Dye Chart

4 parts fuchsia and 1 part yellow: red
1 part red and 1 part yellow: orange
1 part yellow and 2 parts turquoise: green
4 parts turquoise and 1 part fuchsia: blue
2 parts turquoise and 1 part fuchsia: purple

Disco Ball

No 70's Party can be complete without a shiny, spinning disco ball! You can make your own disco ball to decorate your home, garage or party room. You will need an old mirror that you can shatter into small pieces, or you can purchase mirror glass from a crafts store. Carefully break the mirror glass into 2" to 3" pieces by lightly tapping it with a hammer. You will want to have lots of newspaper covering your work surface so you can easily clean up the little glass pieces. It's also a good idea to wear gloves when handling glass so you won't be easily cut by the sharp edges. Next, glue the mirror pieces onto a sphere shaped ball. You can purchase pre-made paper mache spheres, wooden spheres or Styrofoam spheres to adhere the glass pieces to. Make sure to let the glue dry before hanging your disco ball. Give it a spin and shine a light directly at the ball for a groovy effect!

Seventies Music

Have lots of music from the 1970's around your home to play during your party. Some classic groups and artists from the 70's are:

Sly and the Family Stone
Village People
Donna Summer
Elton John
The Commodores
La Chick
KC and The
  Sunshine Band

Kool & the Gang
Average White Band
The Tavres
Patti LaBelle
The Bee Gees
Earth, Wind & Fire
Lionel Richie

Party Planner

My Party Planner

Date of Party_____

Time of Party_____

Guests_____

_____

_____

_____

_____

_____

Party Theme_____

Place/Location_____

Games, Crafts & Activities_____

_____

_____

_____

_____

_____

_____

Foods to Serve _____

_____

_____

_____

_____

Supplies/Food I will need_____

_____

_____

_____

_____

Checklist

❑ Plan Party

❑ Send Invitations

❑ Gather Supplies/Decorations

❑ Purchase/Prepare Food

❑ Chill the Beverages

❑ Decorate for Party

❑ Send Thank You Notes (after party)

My Party Planner

Date of Party_____

Time of Party_____

Guests_____

_____

_____

_____

_____

_____

Party Theme_____

Place/Location_____

Games, Crafts & Activities_____

_____

_____

_____

_____

_____

_____

Foods to Serve _____

_____

_____

_____

_____

Supplies/Food I will need_____

_____

_____

_____

_____

Checklist

❑ Plan Party

❑ Send Invitations

❑ Gather Supplies/Decorations

❑ Purchase/Prepare Food

❑ Chill the Beverages

❑ Decorate for Party

❑ Send Thank You Notes (after party)

My Party Planner

Date of Party_____

Time of Party_____

Guests_____

_____

_____

_____

_____

_____

Party Theme_____

Place/Location_____

Games, Crafts & Activities_____

_____

_____

_____

_____

_____

_____

Foods to Serve _____

_____

_____

_____

_____

Supplies/Food I will need_____

_____

_____

_____

_____

Checklist

❑ Plan Party

❑ Send Invitations

❑ Gather Supplies/Decorations

❑ Purchase/Prepare Food

❑ Chill the Beverages

❑ Decorate for Party

❑ Send Thank You Notes (after party)

My Party Planner

Date of Party_____

Time of Party_____

Guests_____

_____

_____

_____

_____

_____

Party Theme_____

Place/Location_____

Games, Crafts & Activities_____

_____

_____

_____

_____

_____

_____

Foods to Serve _____

_____

_____

_____

_____

Supplies/Food I will need_____

_____

_____

_____

_____

Checklist

❑ Plan Party

❑ Send Invitations

❑ Gather Supplies/Decorations

❑ Purchase/Prepare Food

❑ Chill the Beverages

❑ Decorate for Party

❑ Send Thank You Notes (after party)

My Party Planner

Date of Party_____

Time of Party_____

Guests_____

_____

_____

_____

_____

_____

Party Theme_____

Place/Location_____

Games, Crafts & Activities_____

_____

_____

_____

_____

_____

_____

_____

Foods to Serve _____

_____

_____

_____

_____

Supplies/Food I will need_____

_____

_____

_____

_____

Checklist

❏ Plan Party

❏ Send Invitations

❏ Gather Supplies/Decorations

❏ Purchase/Prepare Food

❏ Chill the Beverages

❏ Decorate for Party

❏ Send Thank You Notes (after party)

My Party Planner

Date of Party_____

Time of Party_____

Guests_____

_____

_____

_____

_____

_____

Party Theme_____

Place/Location_____

Games, Crafts & Activities_____

_____

_____

_____

_____

_____

_____

Foods to Serve _____

_____

_____

_____

_____

Supplies/Food I will need_____

_____

_____

_____

_____

Checklist

❑ Plan Party

❑ Send Invitations

❑ Gather Supplies/Decorations

❑ Purchase/Prepare Food

❑ Chill the Beverages

❑ Decorate for Party

❑ Send Thank You Notes (after party)

Notes

Index

Girls Night

20 Questions 8
Caramel Corn..5
Grabbit...9
Make Your Own Pizzas 3
Orange Creamsicles..3
Pajama Invitations...2
Palm Reading 8
Party Invitations..2
Party Pillows...4
Quiz:Does Your Crush Like You Too?.......................6
Sleeping Bag & Pillow Treats...................................4
Slumber Party Videos..5
Spoons...10
Truth or Dare..9

Spa Night

Apple Slushies 13
Basic Manicure 14
Beauty Rest Invitations..12
Best Lips Contest 18
Cocoa Butter Hand and Nail Treatment...................14
Cosmetic Bag Invitations.......................................12
Funky Face Mask...17
Homemade Cranberry Lip Gloss 15
Lipstick Treasure Hunt...18
Name That Lipstick..18
No Mirror Make-Up...17
Razzle Dazzle Cocktails 13
Spa Jackets..12
Spin the Bottle 16
Sweet Vanilla Lip Balm...15

Fiesta

Cheesy Quesadilla...21
Fiesta Invitations 20
Lime Cooler 22
Make Your Own Piñata 25

Mexicali Popcorn.. 21
Sombrero Cookies... 26
Super Nachos 24
Taco Bar... 23
Taco Invitations... 20
The Best Guacamole 22

Western

Bandana Invitations 28
Bigger Than Texas Invitations 28
Cowboy Boot Invitations...................................... 28
Dazzlin' Bandanas 29
Decorate Cowgirl Hats... 29
Hot Cakes 30
Smiling Cowgirls 32
Southwestern Subs.. 31
Trail Mix Clusters 33
Tumbleweed Cookies 33
Western Mad Lib... 34

Luau

Flamingo Stance Dance.. 41
Flashlight Limbo 42
Flip Flop Invitations 36
Hawaiian Names... 38
Hawaiian Queen... 41
Hula Contest 42
Make Your Own Grass Skirts 39
Mango Tango Smoothie 37
Mini Pineapple Pizzas.. 38
Palm Tree Invitations 36
Paper Leis 40
Sun Tea Punch... 37

Campout

Campfire Apple or Cherry Turnovers 47
Donut Snakes 48
Flashlight Tag.. 49
Marshmallow Invitations 44
Marshmallow Relay 50
Piggly Wiggly 49
Pizza Pockets 46

Silhouettes 50
Sleeping Bag Invitations 44
Survival Kit 45

Movie Star Night

Awards Ceremony 56
Dip for the Stars 57
Make Your Own Film 55
Movie Night Popcorn 54
Movie Star Invitations 52
Movie Ticket Invitations 52
Movie Trivia 58
Name That Star 53
Red Carpet Invitations 52
Who Am I? 53

Sports Party

Blind Man Ball Game 64
Concession Stand 61
Double Dressing 66
Make Your Own Pennant Flags 63
Pennant Flag Invitations 60
Sports Ticket Invitations 60
Strike Three! 65
Ultimate Frisbee 62
You Said It! 64

Mardi Gras

Lots & Lots o' Beads 69
Louisiana Seafood Boil 72
Mardi Gras Invitations 68
Mardi Gras Masks 73
Mask Invitations 68
Original King Cake 70
Shrimp Artichoke Dip 71

Spooky Party

Graveyard Mud Cookies 78
Mr. Kreepy 80
Putrid Punch 77
Scary Noises 81

Spider Web Invitations 76
Squeeze Murder 82
The Mummy Game 81
Tombstone Invitations 76
Worms on a Bun 79

Rock & Roll Party

CD Invitations 84
Chocolate Milk Shakes 85
Elvis' Favorite Sandwich 86
Guitar Invitations 84
Old Fashioned Vanilla Malt 85
Party Dice 90
Root Beer Floats 87
Skating Rink 89
The Best Burgers 88

Beach Party

Beach Cake 93
Beach Kabobs 95
Beach Towel Invitations 92
Fishin' Cupcakes 97
Fruit Smoothies 95
Hang Ten Photos 94
Indoor Beach Party 98
Ocean Cups 96
Seashell Invitations 92
Super Sunglasses 97
Surfboard Invitations 92

70's Night

70's Invitations 100
Disco Ball 106
Funky Straw Art 102
Peace, Love & Happiness 101
Psychedelic Party Mix 104
Rainbow Ice Cream 103
Smiley Face Invitations 100
Tie Dye 105